The Rolls-Royce Story

The Rolls-Royce Story

Reg Abbiss

HX03 BWG

The
History
Press

Published in the United Kingdom in 2012 by
The History Press
The Mill · Brimscombe Port · Stroud · Gloucestershire · GL5 2QG

British Library Cataloguing in Publication Data
A catalogue record for this book is available from the British
Library.

Hardback ISBN 978-0-7524-6614-9

Typesetting and origination by The History Press
Manufacturing managed by Jellyfish Print Solutions Ltd
Printed in India

Half Title page: *The most valuable Rolls-Royce of all, the revered Silver Ghost, AX 201 chassis number 551, celebrated her 100th birthday in 2007. This motor car established the company's reputation for reliability, quality, silence and engineering excellence, and holds many endurance records. With more than half a million miles under her wheels she is regarded by Rolls-Royce engineers as 'just nicely run in'.*

Half Title verso: *The flowing lines of the Silver Seraph, the last saloon made at Crewe, recalled styling cues from the legendary Silver Cloud.*

Title page: *Phantom, 2003, the first car to be produced under BMW's stewardship. A majestic behemoth with more agility than her bulk would suggest.*

➤ *Rolls-Royce Silver Wraith.*

CONTENTS

Rolls-Royce – a name with a touch of magic about it – stands for something special whether you're in London, New York, Beverly Hills or Monte Carlo, and many places in between. The name has a unique place in the lexicon.

The most famous of all motor cars, a Rolls-Royce is instantly recognised by its gleaming radiator grille and statuesque Flying Lady bonnet mascot, and as the gold standard for supreme craftsmanship and engineering excellence.

It lasts a long time. How long? Well, about three-quarters of all Rolls-Royce motor cars built over a century are still on the road or in collections, and able to glide smoothly away when the key is turned.

There has never been anything quite like a Rolls-Royce – a luxurious motor car that you will find wherever you can smell the money. Despite other manufacturers striving mightily for pole position, it remains 'The Rolls-Royce of Motor Cars', as an American automotive journalist described its position in the automotive firmament.

Beautiful names have an ethereal quality to them: Silver Ghost, Phantom, Wraith, Dawn, Shadow, Spirit – a distinguished line of motor cars that have carried heads of state, the mega rich; also average people who took perhaps their only journey in 'The Best Car in the World' to their wedding, or in a Rolls-Royce hearse to their final resting place.

For more than 100 years a Rolls-Royce has been the poster possession of the privileged, the acquisitive, the indulgent and a fair sprinkling of wealthy eccentrics.

A motor car to trigger emotions, envy, pride, avarice, and admiration, though out of reach for 99.9 per cent of those who gaze upon it. Conversely, some call it 'in your face conspicuous consumption'.

However, not all Rolls-Royce owners have the fat wallets of those who lord it over small countries or high finance. Many dedicated enthusiasts devote years to restoring lovingly an old car that they

Did you know?

Hong Kong claims to have more Rolls-Royce cars to the square acre than anywhere else, but for many years the tiny principality of Monaco has claimed more per capita than any country in the world – 300 in a country the size of London's Hyde Park, with a population of 30,000.

will joyfully drive and proudly display at classic car meets. Faced with the choice of heating the garage or the house, the car has been known to win!

Rolls-Royce travel doesn't have to be sedate. In the 1930s Rolls-Royce held world speed records in the air, on land and water and some early heavily armoured Ghosts, weighing 4 tons but capable of beating 50mph, were used by Lawrence of Arabia to wage war. Praising their speed and durability, he said, 'A Rolls in the desert was above rubies'.

This great company, admired the world over for its tremendous achievements in taking engineering forward, has a fascinating history. It brought benefits to millions over many decades with advanced technology, particularly in aviation, though there was a major financial stumble along the way.

Did you know?

Rolls-Royce has long been noted for the quality of its paintwork. Each of the fourteen coats was hand sprayed and then hand rubbed before the next application, and the final protective coating was one and a half times thicker than that on most cars.

Jet engines made Rolls-Royce a world leader in aerospace, but motor cars were the public face. They too struggled financially in the 1990s as car-making economics changed.

Handcrafting only 3,000 cars a year could not generate enough cash for meaningful product development and after a bidding war the car company was split. The manufacture of cars bearing the Rolls-Royce name was transferred to BMW in 2003, while the famed Bentley was bought by Volkswagen. The new owners' deep pockets and huge engineering resources saved both marques from extinction.

Over the twentieth century Rolls-Royce built about 130,000 remarkable carriages, whose like the world will probably not see again.

Their qualities, the soul of Rolls-Royce, I believe, could have sprung only from England, acknowledged the world over for its eccentricities, but also an inbuilt desire to get it right.

Reg Abbiss

Unless otherwise stated, photographs courtesy of:

Rolls-Royce and Bentley Motor Cars;

Rolls-Royce plc;   Sean Kennedy;

British Airways;   Christopher Abbiss;

Jonathan S. Green;   Reg Abbiss.

➤ *Graham Hull's montage of classic Rolls-Royce convertibles.*

ROLLS-ROYCE CONVERTIBLES

1910 ROLLS-ROYCE SILVER GHOST. BY BARKER

1933 ROLLS-ROYCE PHANTOM II. BY JAMES YOUNG

1960 ROLLS-ROYCE SILVER CLOUD. BY H. J. MULLINER

1971 ROLLS-ROYCE CORNICHE

2000 ROLLS-ROYCE CORNICHE

▲ *Allen Swift and his American-built Phantom that he drove almost daily for around three-quarters of a century, setting a world record for owning the same Rolls-Royce longer than anyone else in the world.*

The magic of the name Rolls-Royce stemmed from the partnership of two men whose backgrounds could hardly have been more different. Frederick Henry Royce had to work at the age of ten to help his widowed mother make ends meet. He sold newspapers and delivered telegrams, taught himself engineering, and went on to realise dreams of making mechanical devices work better and last longer. He was a visionary engineer who always called himself simply 'Henry Royce, mechanic'.

The zeal to create the very best of its kind made his name a worldwide benchmark

Charles Stewart Rolls

(1877-1910)

Frederick Henry Royce

(1863-1933)

◄ *Frederick Henry Royce, born in 1863, left school at fourteen and taught himself electrical engineering. He became a great engineer and his name has symbolised excellence for more than a century. Sir Henry Royce died in 1933, having been knighted for his contribution to the British engineering industry. Charles Stewart Rolls brought investment and marketing savvy to the company. An aristocrat who loved to drive fast and to fly, he was among aviation's pioneers and made the first non-stop two-way crossing of the English Channel in 1910.*

C. S. ROLLS & CO.

ROLLS-ROYCE CARS.

10 h.p. R.R. TONNEAU.
Two cylinders.
With Barker body ... ... **£395.**

10 h.p. R.R. PARK PHAETON
With disappearing back seat, leather hood, patent
leather wings, and glass front ... **£436.**

30 h.p. SIX-CYLINDER ROLLS ROYCE CAR.
With Barker side-entrance tonneau ... **£890.**
With Barker six seated limousine ... **£1,000.**

15 h.p. R.R. LANDAULET.
Three cylinders.
With Barker side-entrance tonneau ... **£500.**
Barker single landaulet ... ... **£550.**

20 h.p. R.R. PHAETON de LUXE.
Four cylinders.
With Barker side-entrance tonneau ... **£650.**
Phaeton de Luxe ... ... **£695.**
Extra for Brougham top with extension **£60.**

Telephone
2328, Gerrard

C. S. ROLLS & CO.,

Telephone
104 and 1692, Kens.

28, BROOK ST., BOND ST., W. LILLIE HALL, EARL'S COURT, S.W.

for quality. He established standards and a commitment to excellence that endure today.

His tough childhood was about as far as you could imagine from the aristocratic moneyed world of the man who later became his business partner.

The Honourable Charles Stewart Rolls came from a privileged background, the third son of a wealthy lord, but like Royce also was a visionary. He plunged into

◀ *An advertisement by Charles Rolls' import company in 1904.*

Did you know?

Wheel nuts and bolts of brass were made in-house to ensure not only top quality, but to create left- and right-hand threads to run counter to the direction of travel, so they would never work loose.

the fledgling automotive and aviation worlds, achieving much in a tragically short life, becoming a successful businessman, balloonist, racing car driver and pilot.

Rolls took a mechanical engineering degree at Cambridge while Royce, fourteen years older, was already making his way in the engineering world.

Henry, born in 1863, came from a Lincolnshire family that moved to London in difficult times. He was nine when his father died and he gave up most of his schooling to go to work.

An aunt paid for a railway works apprenticeship in Peterborough, where he also studied electrical engineering, but when she could no longer afford it he walked 100 miles to Leeds for a tool-making job. At nineteen, in 1882, he became chief electrician at an electric company in north-west England.

Two years later he pooled his £20 savings with another engineer, Ernest Claremont, and started a company in Cooke Street,

13

▲ *Charles Rolls at the wheel, with Claude Johnson, known as the hyphen in Rolls-Royce, in a 1905 four-cylinder 20hp.*

Royce and Claremont were so focused on the business that they didn't get out much to meet the young ladies of Manchester, eventually settling for a sort of package deal and marrying two sisters. The company, now making electric cranes, was doing so well in the early 1900s that Royce was able to afford a house in the Knutsford area of Cheshire, making a home there for his mother, who had spent many years in London eking out a living as a housekeeper.

He also bought a car – a French 1901 Decauville – which was noisy, vibrated and had an unreliable electrical system.

Manchester, which soon was making the best electric motors and dynamos in England. One business disadvantage was that they never seemed to wear out, a quality that marked everything Royce was to make.

He decided to make his own car and by late 1903 had designed and built, mostly by himself, the first Royce, with a two-cylinder 10hp engine.

Cheered on by the workforce, he drove out of Cooke Street and, pleased with its smooth performance, drove the 15 miles home.

Now with a reliable car that ran quietly and smoothly, Royce set about improving automobile technology. He designed a carburettor with a throttle arrangement that could be described as the world's first cruise control. He also designed an ignition system and a clutch to provide a smooth take-off, brakes that were much better than anything else on the road and springing to give a good ride.

Rolls, running C.S. Rolls & Company, car importers, in London, wanted to sell a good British car and his partner Claude Johnson, who would become the cement that held the Rolls-Royce Company together and be known as 'the hyphen in Rolls-Royce', persuaded him to go to Manchester to try a Henry Royce car.

Rolls marvelled at the smoothness and quietness of the engine. He knew his search was over.

Royce decided that Rolls was the man to do the marketing and just seven months later, in December 1904, two cars of 10 and 20hp and a 30hp six-cylinder engine won a gold medal at the Paris salon. A contract was signed and Rolls-Royce Ltd was formed in 1906.

Charles Rolls packed much into an exciting life. He set speed records, winning a string of races, and drove a 20hp four-cylinder Rolls-Royce to victory in the Isle of Man 1906 Tourist Trophy race, finishing twenty-seven minutes ahead of the field. He told a motoring reporter who congratulated him: 'The credit is due to Mr. Royce, the designer and builder.'

He then won the Five Miles Silver Trophy for 25hp cars with a 20hp at the Empire

Did you know?
In the quest for quietness and smoothness, Rolls-Royce designed a unique electric gear selector. No push or pull was needed to engage drive or an intermediate gear. A slight pressure on the lever was sufficient for the transmission to respond without fuss or noise.

City raceway, New York. The advanced Royce-designed suspension gave him an edge around the bends and, averaging close to 60mph, he finished twenty seconds ahead of more powerful cars.

The race planted the seed of America's love affair with Rolls-Royce, and led to Rolls setting up a North American import company.

The restless Charles Rolls became a pioneer balloonist, and often crashed as he taught himself to fly a glider.

He learned to pilot a Wright biplane, and in June 1910 made the first non-stop return crossing of the English Channel in a powered aircraft. A month later, a few weeks short of his thirty-third birthday, he was killed at an air show on England's south coast when his plane crashed during a landing competition.

Rolls' death established one more record – the melancholy distinction of being the first Englishman to die in a powered aviation accident.

Royce continued to lead technical development even during years of illness, and worked to the end of his life, bombarding the factory with ideas and drawings.

For somebody committed to doing everything right, he took a surprisingly cavalier attitude toward his own health. He worked too hard for many years – fifteen-hour days were common – and neglected his diet, eating anything that happened to be available, including the junk food of the times, and this took a toll.

Henry Royce was made a Baronet in 1931, a fitting acknowledgement of his contribution to the British motor and aviation industries and to world engineering

standards. One of his favourite sayings reflected his lifelong commitment to engineering excellence: 'Perfection lies in small things. But perfection is no small thing.' He was seventy years old when he died on 22 April 1933.

◄◄ *A cavalcade of classic Rolls-Royce – 100 cars to celebrate the company's centenary.*

◄ *Claude Johnson, managing director, who ran the Rolls-Royce company and kept the company together during Royce's poor health.*

▼ *Charles Rolls, in his Wright biplane, set flying records and was the first Englishman to die in a powered aviation accident, at the age of thirty-two.*

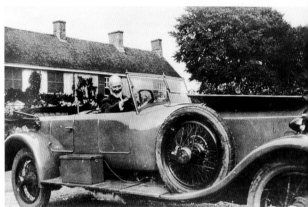

Did you know?

After Henry Royce's death in 1933, the red lettering on the double-R badge on the radiator was changed to black. Mythology has it that this was done as a sign of respect to the founder. Not true. Royce himself had instructed, a short time before, that 'black lettering is more suitable than red to conform to myriad colour schemes'.

◄◄ *Ever the flyer, Rolls in his balloon.*

◄ *Henry Royce in the Phantom prototype at his home in West Wittering, Sussex, in 1925.*

► *Royce with the first experimental Phantom I, which was also his personal car, at Le Canadel, his home on the French Riviera.*

► *Rolls takes the Wright brothers for a spin in the Silver Ghost.*

More than 100 years old, she is called the Silver Ghost, and with half a million miles under her wheels, is the most famous and valuable Rolls-Royce of all. She was Henry Royce's masterpiece and is revered as the flagship that did much to establish the company's reputation for engineering excellence.

▼ 'The Rolls-Royce of Rolls-Royces', the Silver Ghost, the most valuable Rolls-Royce in the world.

One of the few cars driven by both Rolls and Royce, the Silver Ghost broke distance and endurance records, and was hailed by journalists as 'the best car in the world'.

Built on chassis number 551 and bearing the number plate AX 201, she is the only Silver Ghost, though many of the 7,874 Ghosts built over an eighteen-year production run were given the prefix Silver by their owners.

The Silver Ghost's touring Roi des Belges bodywork was by the Barker Company, one of many coachbuilders who fashioned elegant body styles like landaulette, cabriolet, coupé and limousine coachwork, which characterised Rolls-Royce motor cars over the decades.

She shrugs off her age, and like all Rolls-Royce motor cars is meant to be driven spiritedly. Going back as far as the era of the

Wright brothers, who were given a trip out in her by Charles Rolls, she is entitled to be treated respectfully, but the company has never hesitated to drive her in city traffic.

She has faced rush hour in New York and downtown Boston, Los Angeles freeways, and even the fearsome New Jersey and Pennsylvania turnpikes.

Her 40/50hp engine comes to life with a swing of the starting handle and though weighing nearly 2 tons with passengers and luggage, she has been timed over a flying quarter mile at 53mph.

Her carriage lamps and other fittings are silver plated and with the coachwork finished in aluminium paint, the Silver

Did you know?
The length of a Rolls-Royce Phantom – 19ft – was used to determine the space between British parking meters.

◀ *Phantom I Sedanca de Ville by Hooper.*

Ghost was used to tell the world about Henry Royce's remarkable cars.

Fast and quiet, the Silver Ghost was technically superior to anything on the road. *Autocar* magazine, in April 1907, eulogised that she was the smoothest car they had ever experienced and a reference to the loudest sound being the clock inspired the famous 'ticking of the clock' Silver Cloud advertising half a century later.

▼ *Phantom II sports saloon.*

Charles Rolls and managing director Claude Johnson, a natural publicist, took the car on rough hill climbs and long runs to prove her mettle, setting records for speed and stamina. Her most notable trip was an unprecedented 15,000-mile run, back and forth, between London and Glasgow, which doubled the existing long-distance record, and more than 14,300 miles of the marathon were completed without an involuntary stop. Halfway through, when the Ghost broke the 7,089-mile reliability record, the company produced a poster proclaiming: 'The Worlds Record for a Non-Stop Motor Run Broken'.

The Silver Ghost was driven by a private owner for forty years, then came home to the company in 1949 in part exchange for a Rolls-Royce.

For its first forty years in business, Rolls-Royce did not build a complete car, making the chassis, engine and technical components, then sending it to coachbuilders to complete the owner's requirements.

AFTER THE GHOSTS – THE PHANTOMS

The solidly built Ghosts were so versatile that it was unnecessary to make anything

▼ *Phantom IV landaulette, 1950–56, in London on a quiet morning.*

► *World record broken.*

Did you know?

To demonstrate the smoothness of the engine of his 1907 masterpiece, the Silver Ghost, Henry Royce would balance a penny on the radiator while the engine was running.

THE WORLDS RECORD FOR A NON-STOP MOTOR RUN BROKEN

MR CLAUDE JOHNSON.
COMMERCIAL MANAGING DIRECTOR
OF THE Cº WHO ORIGINATED AND
ORGAINISED THE TRIAL.
AND WHO HAS
DRIVEN 2635 ⅜
MILES TO DATE.

MR F.H. ROYCE.
THE DESIGNER OF THE CAR AND
ENGINEER IN CHIEF OF THE Cº.

THE HON. C.S. ROLLS
TECHNICAL MANAGING DIRECTOR
OF THE Cº

WHO HAS
DRIVEN
1249 ½ MILES
TO DATE.

CHIEF TESTOR PLATFORD.
WHO PREPARED THE CAR FOR THE
TRIAL. AND WHO HAS DRIVEN
2629 ¼ MILES TO DATE.

THE "SILVER GHOST"
THE 6 CYLINDER ROLLS ROYCE CAR WHICH ON
FRIDAY LAST COMPLETED 7214 MILES NON STOP IN
AN OFFICIAL ROAD TRIAL UNDER THE ROYAL
AUTOMOBILE CLUB AND WHICH IS STILL RUNNING
400 MILES PER DAY BETWEEN LONDON AND
GLASGOW

MECHANICIAN MACREADY.
WHO HAS DRIVEN
1329 ¼ MILES TO DATE.

else until the 1920s, when the company thought it prudent to offer a smaller alternative. A 20hp Baby Rolls came out in late 1922 and 2,940 were built over seven years. The Ghost, which sold more than 8,414 over an eighteen-year production

ROLLS ROYCE

THE BEST SIX-CYLINDER CAR IN THE WORLD?

A FEW REASONS WHY THE ROLLS-ROYCE IS THE BEST SIX-CYLINDER CAR IN THE WORLD.

Because of its

(1) Flexibility.
(2) Lightness and cheapness in tyres.
(3) Reliability.
(4) Silence.
(5) Efficiency and cheapness in upkeep.
(6) Safety—brakes, steering gear, etc.
(7) Ease of manipulation, lightness of steering, clutch operation, etc.

A private owner of a R.R. writes :

"I may say my car is a perfect dream. It is so reliable that I have done away with my carriages and horses."

The original of this letter and many other letters from private owners of Rolls Royce cars may be seen at

ROLLS-ROYCE, Ltd.,

14 & 15, CONDUIT STREET, LONDON, W.

Telegrams : "Rolhead, London."   Telephones {487 } Gerrard {1494 }

AGENTS for LEICESTER, NOTTINGHAM, RUTLAND, AND DERBYSHIRE
AGENTS for NORTH RIDING OF YORKSHIRE AND DURHAM
AGENTS, FRANCE
AGENTS, UNITED STATES OF AMERICA
AGENTS, OTTAWA (CANADA) and DISTRICT

The Midland Counties Motor Garage Co., Granby Street, Leicester
The Cleveland Car Co., Cleveland Bridge Works, Darlington.
La Société Anonyme "L'Eclaire," 66, Rue la Boétie, Paris.
The Rolls-Royce Import Co., Broadway, New York
Messrs. Ketchum & Co., corner of Bank St. and Sparks St., Ottawa

28

span, was superseded in 1925 by the 40/50hp Phantom I, to be followed in 1929 by Phantom II with an improved suspension.

Phantom III emerged in 1935 with a mighty twelve-cylinder engine, a top speed of 100mph and an independent front suspension, a formidable package that stayed in production until the start of the Second World War.

A smaller model, the Wraith, the quietest Rolls-Royce to date, came out in 1938. Then, when the Crewe aero engine factory switched to motor cars after the war, the Silver Dawn, in 1949, was the first complete car to be built by Rolls-Royce.

Phantom IV, which began production five years after the Second World War, was super exclusive, even by Rolls-Royce

Rolls-Royce never missed an opportunity to remind the world of the ultimate accolade.

➤ *Phantom VI was hand built by the Rolls-Royce Mulliner Park Ward Division and offered exceptional comfort for up to seven passengers.*

standards, some being beautifully styled landaulettes sporting coats of arms. Only eighteen were produced, for royalty and heads of state.

THE QUEEN'S PHANTOMS

Only in Britain, anglophiles will marvel, will you find a quintet of Rolls-Royce Phantom limousines alongside ornate horse-drawn state coaches, decorated with gold leaf.

Parked in the Royal Mews at Buckingham Palace are more than 100 coaches and carriages – a unique collection spanning 300 years of the coachbuilder's art and still used for ceremonial occasions. Mostly, however, HM the Queen opts for a Phantom limousine, an impressive behemoth of great presence with huge windows, and standing regally tall.

The oldest, a Phantom IV, ordered when she was Princess Elizabeth, is of such an age that it was carrying the future queen years before the Beatles shot to fame. She belies her bulk by being able to clock 100mph.

▲ *Phantom V saloon by James Young.*

➤ *Queen Elizabeth in a royal open Phantom.*

➤➤ *Royal Phantoms at Buckingham Palace.*

She was joined by a Phantom V landaulette, built in the early 1960s, and later by two Phantom VI state limousines representing everything symbolic about Rolls-Royce.

To ensure crowds a good view, they were fitted with a transparent dome and sunroof, and as the queen is petite, powered rear seats.

The royal Phantoms have a different Spirit of Ecstasy. She is in a kneeling position, a variant not seen since the 1950s. This triggered a fuss when the Saudis ordered a dozen Rolls-Royce with the kneeling lady. The company was accused of chauvinism for producing 'a subservient woman to make Arab buyers feel macho'.

The queen also has a personal bonnet mascot, which appears on her limousine on state occasions: a solid silver miniature sculpture of St George slaying the dragon.

Did you know?
Rolls-Royce was the first to put heated rear windows into cars.

Phantom buyers could expect the bill to travel well north of half a million pounds, depending on how far over the top with luxurious extras they wished to go. Little wonder, considering the work involved. The only Rolls-Royce to retain a separate chassis and using age-old coach-building techniques, Phantoms required fourteen months' work – sometimes longer if the customer specified extras like cocktail cabinets, a miniature home theatre or the faces of Rolls and Royce outlined in marquetry on the ceiling.

Mallets and metal rollers were used to shape the body, creating subtle curves and sweeping coach lines, and hand and eye made the judgement calls as often as measuring instruments.

In 1959 it was decided that ordinary mortals could order the new Phantom V, and 832 were built before the last of the great line, the seven-seat Phantom VI, emerged in 1968.

Stylish and elegant, the 'P Six' was a classic – everyone's idea of a true Rolls-Royce limousine.

The Phantom series cruised to the longest run of any Rolls-Royce model, 6,700 being built between 1925 and the 1990s.

A stroll among the hundreds of Rolls-Royce cars at the annual rally of the enthusiasts' club on an English summer's day is to walk through the company's history. It is an impressive sight.

THE CLOUDS EMERGE FROM THE PHANTOMS

If you were to ask people to draw a Rolls-Royce, they would likely try to come up with the flowing lines of the Silver Cloud, and that would be a tip of the hat to the man who designed it, John Blatchley, who has been referred to as the shaper of the modern Rolls-Royce for the Cloud and its successor, the Silver Shadow.

Many believe the Silver Cloud, introduced in 1955 and produced for just over ten years, was the most beautiful Rolls-Royce saloon car of all.

Of 14,659 built, about half were Bentleys, which were identical, apart from the radiator grille and badging.

Few models have achieved the admiration commanded by the Silver Cloud, though the Corniche convertible might run close to it.

The Cloud promised performance as well as style: its six-cylinder engine would take it to 100mph. Cloud II, in 1959, came with a more powerful V8 engine and

The Rolls-Royce Silver Cloud – $13,995

"At 60 miles an hour the loudest noise in this new Rolls-Royce comes from the electric clock"

*What makes Rolls-Royce the best car in the world? "There is really no magic about it—
it is merely patient attention to detail," says an eminent Rolls-Royce engineer.*

1. "At 60 miles an hour the loudest noise comes from the electric clock," reports the Technical Editor of THE MOTOR. Three mufflers tune out sound frequencies—acoustically.

2. Every Rolls-Royce engine is run for seven hours at full throttle before installation, and each car is test-driven for hundreds of miles over varying road surfaces.

3. The Rolls-Royce is designed as an owner-driven car. It is eighteen inches shorter than the largest domestic cars.

4. The car has power steering, power brakes and automatic gear-shift. It is very easy to drive and to park. No chauffeur required.

5. The finished car spends a week in the final test-shop, being fine-tuned. Here it is subjected to 98 separate ordeals. For example, the engineers use a stethoscope to listen for axle-whine.

6. The Rolls-Royce is guaranteed for three

years. With a new network of dealers and parts-depots from Coast to Coast, service is no problem.

7. The Rolls-Royce radiator has never changed, except that when Sir Henry Royce died in 1933 the monogram RR was changed from red to black.

8. The coachwork is given five coats of primer paint, and hand rubbed between each coat, before nine coats of finishing paint go on.

9. By moving a switch on the steering column, you can adjust the shock-absorbers to suit road conditions.

10. A picnic table, veneered in French walnut, slides out from under the dash. Two more swing out behind the front seats.

11. You can get such optional extras as an Espresso coffee-making machine, a dictating machine, a bed, hot and cold water for washing, an electric razor or a telephone.

12. There are three separate systems of power brakes, two hydraulic and one mechanical. Damage to one system will not affect the others. The Rolls-Royce is a very safe car—and also a very lively car. It cruises serenely at eighty-five. Top speed is in excess of 100 m.p.h.

13. The Bentley is made by Rolls-Royce. Except for the radiators, they are identical motor cars, manufactured by the same engineers in the same works. People who feel diffident about driving a Rolls-Royce can buy a Bentley.

PRICE. The Rolls-Royce illustrated in this advertisement—f.o.b. principal ports of entry—costs **$13,995.**

If you would like the rewarding experience of driving a Rolls-Royce or Bentley, write or telephone to one of the dealers listed on the opposite page.

Rolls-Royce Inc., 10 Rockefeller Plaza, New York 20, N. Y., CIrcle 5-1144.

An advertisement reprinted from FORTUNE, March, 1959.

standard automatic transmission. Further mechanical refinement gave Cloud III, in 1962, a top speed approaching 120mph.

Silver Clouds exemplified everything about Rolls-Royce style and refinement, and they are revered to this day.

Did you know?

Though looking to the future, Rolls-Royce always acknowledged the past. In the early 1970s, Charles W. Ward, director of the Mulliner Park Ward coach-building division, said: 'We are moving toward light alloy aircraft-type construction although the craftsmanship of our men is inherited directly from the days of coaches drawn by six horses with postillions in knee breeches.'

◄ *The legendary Silver Cloud ticking of the clock advertisement.*

► *A Silver Wraith sports saloon (1947–59), the first post-Second World War car made at Crewe.*

The beautiful Silver Cloud, produced from 1955–66. The Rolls-Royce show car at the New York Motor Show in 1958 was Radford Countryman Silver Cloud, modified for gentlemanly pursuits like horseracing. The boot doubled as an observation platform and the car had cooking facilities, including hot water.

A Rolls-Royce has always exemplified world-class engineering and craftspeople whose skills with wood and leather have created motor cars sometimes described as mobile Rembrandts.

The most famous radiator in the world required supreme skill with a little help with illusion from the ancient Greeks. The lines, apparently straight and flat, are in fact slightly curved.

The Greeks called this geometric distortion *entasis* and the principle was applied to the columns of the Parthenon, probably Greece's most famous symbol. Legend has it that Charles Rolls climbed to the summit of the Acropolis, and the soaring columns of the Greek temple inspired the design of the grille that became a hallmark of the motor cars.

For decades, only ten men in the world knew how to craft a Rolls-Royce radiator, each one taking a day to make. Most of them served the company for more than a quarter century, and trained apprentices to be their successors.

Seemingly silver, the mirror-finish came from five hours of polishing the steel until it gleamed brighter than chrome and, in addition to the double-R badge at the front, each grille bore a secret second set of initials, the craftsman's own – a signature by which he took personal responsibility for his work.

Tony Kent, who made about 4,000 radiators over his career, told me: 'The finest joints we can hope to get are about the thickness of a human hair. That's what we aim for.'

Did you know?
Only one hide in twelve passed Rolls-Royce upholstery quality leather requirements. The rejects were sold to make expensive handbags.

Did you know?
Each Rolls-Royce
had a history book,
detailing the work
done over the twelve-
week build process.
Every engineer and
craftsman initialled
his work to confirm
completion.

➤ *The handcrafted
Rolls-Royce radiator
grille.*

Such detailed handcrafting helps explain the high costs of quality and workmanship that sets a Rolls-Royce apart from all others.

IS THAT A WOMAN IN HER NIGHTIE ON THE FRONT OF YOUR CAR?

After the RR badge was soldered to the front of the radiator, one task remained – the fitting of the Spirit of Ecstasy. The model for the racy statuette was Miss Eleanor Thornton, a lady in her early twenties who was believed to be the mistress as well as personal assistant to the Honourable John Scott-Montagu, whose ancestral Hampshire estate today houses the Beaulieu classic car collection.

The mildly erotic Flying Lady, which was to become the Rolls-Royce symbol, slightly shocked Edwardian England and nobody stepped forward at the time to admit, 'It is I'.

After a year or two, word suggested that the model was Eleanor Thornton, an unusually liberated young lady for her time.

sought an elegant figurehead conveying speed, silence and grace.

The designer, Charles Sykes of the Royal Academy, said he 'experienced a spirit of

Sadly, she died along with 334 passengers and crew when the P&O liner *Persia* was torpedoed by a U-boat off the coast of Crete.

'Nellie in her nightie', as owners referred to the Flying Lady, came about when Rolls-Royce, concerned about frivolous ornaments attached to radiator caps,

◄ *Tony Kent, one of the few men in the world with the skill to handcraft a gleaming Rolls-Royce radiator grille of stainless steel. Each one required a day's work.*

◄ *Eleanor Thornton, the model for the Spirit of Ecstasy.*

➤ *Rolls-Royce photographer Richard Smiles took this innovative photograph beneath the towers of the World Trade Centre.*

➤➤ *Wax model of the bonnet mascot.*

ecstasy' during a drive in Montagu's 40/50 Ghost.

He had a vision of 'a graceful figure on the prow of a Rolls-Royce revelling in the freshness of the air and the musical sound of her fluttering veils – arms outstretched and her sight fixed upon the distance'.

Eleanor first appeared atop the radiator in February 1911, and has symbolised Rolls-Royce ever since, though over eight

decades she was reduced from her initial height of 7in to 4in. Sadly, the fun-loving Charles Rolls never experienced the pleasure of gazing down the long bonnet at the beautiful creature that exhilarated Sykes. Rolls' fatal air crash had occurred seven months previously.

◄ *The kneeling Spirit of Ecstasy, which has attracted controversy at times.*

▼ *The Spirit of Ecstasy in all her glory.*

metal was poured and the plaster was chipped away to reveal a replica of the original wax figure, precise in every detail.

HALLMARKS

Rolls-Royce interiors have always been noted for beautiful woodwork and leather upholstery, matched only by Crewe Bentleys.

The striking natural beauty of burr walnut veneer covering the fascia and waist rails was highlighted by master craftsmen, who skilfully cut and matched the patterns before lacquering and polishing the wood to a glass-like finish.

The statuette was cast in stainless steel, using the lost wax process that was invented by the Chinese to produce works of art 4,000 years ago. A wax model was covered with plaster and heated to 1,000°C. The melted wax left a cavity into which molten

A dozen cowhides, carefully matched for colour and texture, covered the upholstery, 250 pieces of Connolly leather being hand-cut and sewn for each seat. This is where the ladies of Rolls-Royce added their skills.

▲► *The coach-built Corniche, regarded by many as the most beautiful convertible Rolls-Royce ever built.*

Sewing machines played a part, but nimble fingers were needed for intricate tailoring and fitting.

Just as the wood and leather benefited from expertise passed down through decades, so with the luxurious carpeting from mills that were weaving the highest quality Wilton before Victoria became Queen of the British Empire, using some looms that had been used for centuries.

Observe the engineering and metal-crafting skills, leather and veneer artisans, and you have an idea why about seven out of ten motor cars bearing the names of Henry Royce and Charles Rolls are still around today.

▲ The beautiful leather upholstery in the Silver Spur passenger compartment.

Did you know?

The beautiful double lines running from the front to the back of Rolls-Royce coachwork were applied by a craftsman who would dip a fine brush into the paint until he had just the right amount, squint along the car's waistline and, without pausing, apply two remarkably straight lines. It was such personal handiwork that gave the motor car its special character.

◀ ▶ *No manufacturer in the world could expect to match the glorious Phantom state landaulette versions of the Phantom V and VI, which were built only for heads of state.*

'When you enter this motor car,' Fritz Feller, chief engineer for styling and future projects, told a journalist, 'you are in a different world. Many cars are faster, some are sportier to handle. But that's not what this car is about. It's like entering a drawing room – a feeling of remoteness from the rest of the world, from everyday cares, that makes a Rolls-Royce different from all other cars.'

Fritz, a delightful gnome-like man, born in Austria, came to England as a boy and loved Rolls-Royce possibly more than most of the British.

His handiwork on Rolls-Royce classics, spanning more than forty years, spoke to the values and commitment to getting it right that motivated the highly skilled people behind the name.

Rolls-Royce has always believed in evolution rather than revolution, making changes only when a definite benefit was identified, and after exhaustive testing over 50,000 miles. A new model, true to the heritage, had to be a logical and natural successor, appearing only when it was deemed to be right.

▼ *Checking that each wire does what it should and is in the right place.*

Did you know?
Meticulous attention to detail at Rolls-Royce included running fingertips over the paintwork as though reading Braille to seek any imperfection.

The journalist Don Vorderman wrote, 'The leather, veneers and carpeting set the tone for an unsurpassed travel experience; setting a Rolls-Royce apart from mere mortals.'

Many elements came together to create motor cars of distinctive yet understated styling, and a unique presence. Fritz Feller would say, 'We will have succeeded in our

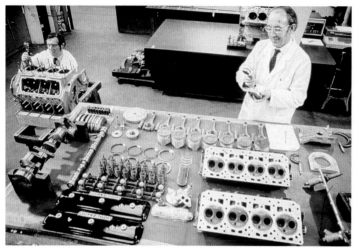

Henry Royce was to producing the finest motor cars human ingenuity could achieve. They applied artistry to coach building and the finest natural materials.

All engine building was by hand from the start – at the first workshops in Cooke Street, Manchester, in the early 1900s, when production moved to Derby in 1908, and later at Crewe, which switched to car manufacturing after the Second World War.

There the engines were built in workshops where components for wartime Merlin aero engines had been precision machined. The same tolerances, to ten-thousandths of an inch, were stipulated for the motor car.

One engineer took final responsibility for each engine, which was run for two hours on test beds, with particular attention to quietness and vibration during which a

One engine in 100 is disassembled after rigorous bench testing and checked for wear or imperfections.

task if late on a winter's evening someone catches a glimpse of a travel-stained car and says "A Rolls-Royce has just gone by".'

A Rolls-Royce is a magical blend of form and function created by talented craftspeople and engineers, as dedicated as

◄◄ Though the collision was severe, the tank-like front structure of a Silver Shadow absorbed the impact so well that all the doors would still open and the driver was able to walk away.

◄ The beauty of interior craftsmanship in veneer and leather.

specialist listened for unusual noises with a stethoscope.

One engine in every hundred was taken to the lab and put through a punishing twenty-hour test cycle, then stripped and every piece microscopically examined for signs of wear. The engine was then reassembled and sent to the production line that moved but a few feet each day.

Before others thought about it, Rolls-Royce was fitting two, and for a time, three independent braking systems. If something failed, the car would still have four-wheel stopping power. The extra work and expense were irrelevant.

The 1924 Ghost had an anti-lock servo-system, not unlike one advertised as 'a major technological advance' by a German

◄ The 'Dobson-family-Royce'. Derek Dobson, his son and five brothers, who between them served 211 years at Rolls-Royce Motor Cars.

▲ Skilfully matched and cut Lombardian walnut veneers grace the completed instrument panel of a Corniche II.

➤ The Rolls-Royce 'birth certificate', the history book, chronicles every stage of the car's manufacture.

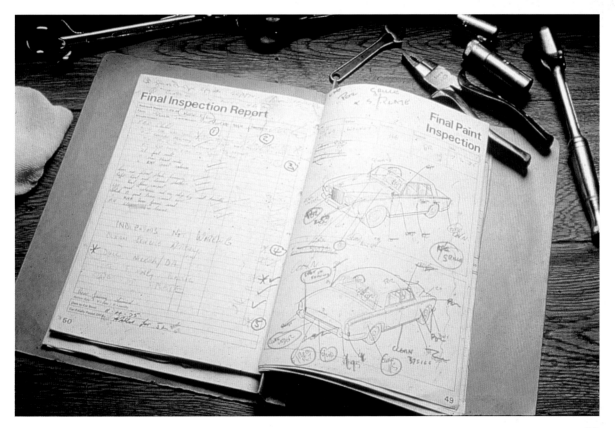

53

manufacturer sixty-four years later. Rolls-Royce sometimes was way ahead of the engineering game.

Body shells were submerged repeatedly in anti-corrosion primers to form a weather-resistant barrier almost impervious to water – a prelude to fourteen coats of lacquer, hand sprayed and rubbed to provide gleaming paintwork to last many years.

A quiet interior has always been mandatory, ensuring that every word could be heard at 120mph.

The Rolls-Royce motor cars of Derby and Crewe, some now many decades old, are running today because the mantra called for engineering integrity and the finest materials.

The essence of a Rolls-Royce, however, its heart and soul, has always been its people:

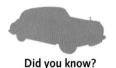

Did you know?
An early Rolls-Royce catalogue stated: Doctors have declared that the Rolls-Royce is the only petrol car that they can bring to a patient's house and drive away without disturbing the patient.

Did you know?
The Rolls-Royce exhaust system was acoustically tuned to suppress a wide range of sound frequencies and every motor car was driven for 100 miles on the roads and lanes of Cheshire, to check that the sound-proofing met company standards for quiet, restful travel.

talented craftsmen and women who poured their skills into creating a beautiful machine, and then passed those skills on.

They were, and are, the DNA of Rolls-Royce.

Ten years into making the best cars on the road, Henry Royce spread his wings, designing aircraft engines that propelled Rolls-Royce to world leadership.

He was asked to make engines for British warplanes as the First World War got under way, and within a year designed and built the Eagle, a power unit superior to anything in the air. When the war ended in 1918 almost two thirds of the engines in British aircraft were Rolls-Royce.

Royce had a genius for developing engines that generated significantly more power than originally designed into them. The Eagle was the first of a range that, despite his failing health, he designed over the following eighteen years.

Two Eagle engines, in June 1919, carried the British flyers James Alcock and Arthur Whitten Brown in a converted Vickers Vimy bomber on the first non-stop crossing of the Atlantic by air – Newfoundland to Ireland, 1,890 miles – in sixteen hours, twenty-seven minutes.

A larger engine, the R, broke world speed records in the air, on water and on land in the thirties, including winning the International Schneider Trophy air race three years running. The R, developed to achieve more than twice its original power and raising the world air speed record to 407mph in a Supermarine S6 seaplane in 1931, powered the racing boats of Henry Segrave and Kaye Don to water speed records, and propelled Malcolm Campbell's *Bluebird* to a 272mph land speed record at Daytona Beach in 1933. It pushed the record beyond 300mph two years later.

Thunderbolt, a Rolls-Royce-powered monster of a car weighing 6 tons and generating 4,700hp, was driven by George Eyston at 357mph to another land-speed record on the Bonneville flats in Utah in 1938.

Henry Royce's magnificent R engine led to the Merlin, which powered the Battle of Britain Spitfires and Hurricanes, as well as the Lancaster bombers that inflicted much damage on Britain's enemies in the Second World War.

With another war on the way in 1938, Rolls-Royce built a factory to produce the Merlin, at Crewe in Cheshire. Within fourteen weeks of breaking ground, parts were being made and the factory built 26,000 of the 166,000 Rolls-Royce Merlins produced by 1945. The versatile engine also went into tanks and motor torpedo boats, and its power curve was continually boosted to stay ahead of the Germans.

The Merlin was Henry Royce's greatest gift to the most important cause of all, though he did not live to savour its triumphs.

LET'S BUILD A JET ENGINE

Of the many advanced technology engines that have been built by Rolls-Royce, the most historic has to be the development of a revolutionary gas turbine, invented by Frank Whittle, a brilliant twenty-two-year-old RAF engineer. It was the genesis of the jet engine that was to change aviation history dramatically.

Hundreds of Rolls-Royce engineers worked on the project and within months, in May 1941, the Whittle W1 jet engine flew in a Gloster E28 experimental plane. It went into service in Gloster Meteor fighters in 1944, just before the end of the war, and the following year it set a 606mph speed record.

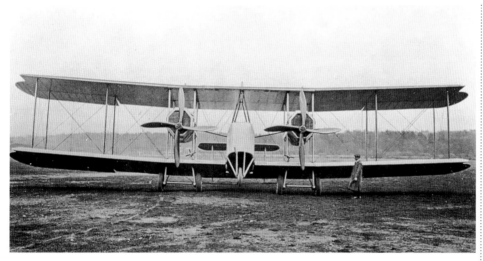

In March 1956 British test pilot Peter Twiss became the first man officially to exceed 1,000mph in level flight. His Fairey Delta research plane, powered by a Rolls-Royce Avon turbojet, set a world aviation speed record of 1,132mph.

Whittle's visionary turbine power unit led to the development of military jets, including the Pegasus, for the Harrier vertical take-off fighter, and Avon engines for the first jetliner, the de Havilland Comet, and other British passenger aircraft.

➤ *The famed Merlin that powered RAF Spitfire and Hurricane fighters and bombers in the Second World War and is credited with winning the Battle of Britain.*

◀ The Rolls-Royce factory at Crewe, built at record speed in 1938 to make the Merlin engine, which defeated the Luftwaffe, and turned to making motor cars after the war.

The Rolls-Royce-powered Supermarine won the International Schneider Trophy three years running to win the trophy outright.

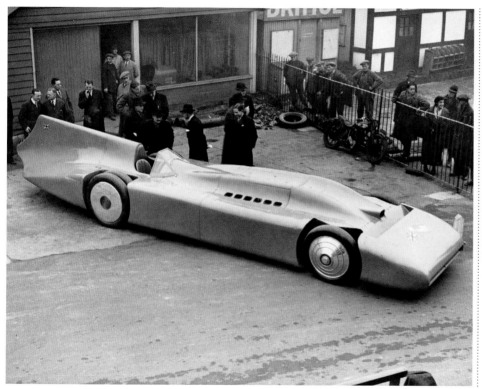

◄ *Sir Malcolm Campbell's* Bluebird *race car broke world speed records.*

◄◄ *Early Whittle experimental jet engine.*

◄ *First flight of the Whittle jet engine in the Gloster E28 experimental jet fighter.*

The Rolls-Royce double-R badge has adorned high-performance engines in generations of airliners, from the Boeing 707 and Douglas DC8 to the supersonic Concorde, Boeing 747, Boeing 787 Dream liner, the mammoth double-deck Airbus A380 and the Airbus A340, which can fly for eighteen hours non-stop, beyond perhaps even the dreams of Henry Royce and Frank Whittle.

Henry Royce set supreme engineering standards for entire industries, transforming the motor car from a clanking, temperamental contraption into a safe, smooth, practical means of transport. He also pioneered aircraft engines that won wars and opened up travel to millions.

He always believed that what was already done well could be made even better. There was only one way to approach a task; compromise was unthinkable.

His many accomplishments could give rise to a multitude of epitaphs. The great

◄ *Rolls-Royce RB-211-powered British Airways 747.*

Did you know?

A London businessman in a hurry set a world speed record from London to New York using only Rolls-Royce power: Concorde, two helicopters and two cars. The time: four hours, twenty-three minutes, office to office.

► *The beloved Spitfire, this one owned by Rolls-Royce plc.*

◄ *Harrier jump jet powered by Rolls-Royce Pegasus engine.*

▶ *The Silver Ghost at Sydney International Airport, with a Rolls-Royce-powered Qantas Boeing 747. Dennis Miller-Williams, the London public relations manager, is at the wheel of the world's most famous Rolls-Royce, while the author stands in the air intake of the RB-211 engine to give an idea of its size.*

engineer would perhaps be content with something written by Ronald W. Harker in his 1979 book, *The Engines were Rolls-Royce*:

The name Rolls-Royce stands not only for excellence but for honest endeavour, fair trading and good behaviour. It is a name to conjure with; one for future generations to revere and emulate.

➤ *Henry Royce, Charles Rolls and symbols of their legacy. (Jonathan S. Green, Rolls-Royce plc)*

◄◄◄ A classic coach-built H.J. Mulliner Silver Wraith 1956 touring limousine built for the Maharani of Baroda. Now owned by Sean Kennedy of Wynnewood, Pennsylvania.

◄◄ The flowing lines of the Silver Seraph, the last saloon made at Crewe, recalled styling cues from the legendary Silver Cloud.

◄ The elegant and stylish Silver Cloud, which many consider to be the most beautiful Rolls-Royce saloon of all.

➤ 'A Rolls in the desert was above rubies,' said Lawrence of Arabia of his fleet of 40/50hp armoured Rolls-Royce Ghosts.

Rolls-Royce bankrupt! It happened with chilling suddenness on 4 February 1971. The blow to national self-esteem hit like a shockwave.

Britain's most revered company had gone bust. The problem wasn't the fabled motor car, it was the dominant aerospace division, whose ambitious project to make the world's most advanced high-thrust jet engine, the RB-211 for the Lockheed Tri-Star airliner, had hit the wall.

Rolls-Royce had cut its price to the bone to beat American competitors to the prize of being the Tri-Star's sole engine supplier. Too much, it turned out, as technical problems caused delays and sent costs soaring.

The money had run out, and in British law you call in a receiver if you can't meet the payroll. The receiver now effectively owned Rolls-Royce, and in his hands was an industrial dynasty and the jobs of 80,000 people.

The news was likened to the Bank of England closing its doors. People who had never ridden in a Rolls-Royce but were proud of its stellar reputation were appalled.

An official at Lockheed's London office said dryly, 'If Rolls-Royce is bust, we've got the biggest fleet of gliders in aviation history.'

Rolls-Royce was more than a company in the psyche of the British. It made 'the best cars in the world', its Merlin engines defeated the Luftwaffe in the Battle of Britain and it was a world leader in jet engine technology.

I was then the BBC's Industrial Correspondent, and as I covered the

Did you know?
Eighty thousand components went into every Rolls-Royce, many being produced in the factory machine shop to ensure top quality. The result was a motor car with several times the lifespan of an ordinary car.

► *Battle of Britain pilot at the Derby factory.*

story I pictured the inspirational Memorial Window at the Rolls-Royce Derby factory.

Depicting a young airman in leather jacket and flying boots, atop a Merlin engine, the moving inscription read:

THIS WINDOW COMMEMORATES THE PILOTS OF THE ROYAL AIR FORCE WHO IN THE BATTLE OF BRITAIN, TURNED THE WORK OF OUR HANDS INTO THE SALVATION OF OUR COUNTRY

Thirty years or so later, the company's own salvation was now in serious question.

The RB-211 required modifications costing millions from already strained budgets, and there was a major setback when the carbon-fibre main fan blade of the massive engine failed bird-strike impact testing. This

meant switching to titanium, adding weight to each engine. Engineers needed more time and money. Behind schedule and with Lockheed already building the Tri-Star, there was too little of either.

The receiver, Rupert Nicholson, a senior partner at an international accountancy firm, told journalists that a new deal would have to be negotiated with Lockheed if the project was to have a future. He would do everything he could to salvage the engine programme, preserve jobs and save the Rolls-Royce car and diesel divisions.

The British government, aware of the cash problems, had agreed to cover most of the increased engineering costs with about £60 million of public and private financing, subject to an independent audit. This was still pending when the company ran out of money.

The government feared that an open-ended commitment would expose taxpayers to huge debts and compensation claims from Lockheed and the airlines.

In this scenario, the car division was a blip on the radar. The most critical issue was the aerospace operation, tens of thousands of jobs and the repercussions of Britain's mightiest engineering company reneging on international commitments to airlines, air forces, navies and power generation.

Facing up to political and commercial reality, the government agreed to a rescue plan that would keep Britain in the world aerospace league, and reassure governments and commercial customers that Rolls-Royce would be there to meet its commitments.

Lockheed, also cash-strapped, secured loan guarantees from the US government.

➤ RB-211 engines doing Rolls-Royce proud.

Did you know?
A grateful patient so appreciated her surgeon's life-saving work that she went straight to the New York City dealer upon leaving hospital, bought a Rolls-Royce and had it delivered to the hospital front entrance with a letter saying simply: Thank you.

Rolls-Royce was divided into two companies. The biggest chunk, the aerospace, marine and industrial turbine divisions which made engines not only for jetliners and military aircraft, but ships, nuclear submarines, power stations and

◄ The massive Trent jets developed from the RB-211 on the wing of an Airbus A380.

oilfield pipelines, was sold to the British government for £1 and named Rolls-Royce (1971) Ltd. The car and diesel divisions were spun into a new company, Rolls-Royce Motors.

Rupert Nicholson's accomplishment was outstanding, and is regarded by many as a receivership classic. When he began sorting out the corporate wreckage, the shares stood at only a few pennies.

He set the aerospace company on course to a profitable new era and secured a future for Rolls-Royce Motors Ltd, which was floated on the stock exchange two years after the collapse. For the original shareholders he achieved a payout of 58p – nearly $1 per share. How many stockholders, skewered when a firm goes bankrupt, wind up with anything?

Many thousands of jobs were saved and a future mapped out for not one but two firms bearing the most illustrious name in engineering.

Rupert Nicholson was the honoured guest in 1979 when Rolls-Royce Motors held a seventy-fifth anniversary lunch at the Midland Hotel in Manchester to mark the historic meeting of Henry Royce and Charles Rolls in the very same dining room. He beamed, reflecting perhaps that accountancy could border on the exciting after all.

Ultimately, the enormous potential of the RB-211 engine that brought Rolls-Royce down in 1971 was realised. Its performance was enhanced over the following forty years to generate a mighty thrust exceeding 100,000lb – more than three times the original design power output. Arguably the outstanding jumbo jet engine of the twentieth century, its technology was the genesis of the huge Trent 900 engine built by Rolls-Royce for the gigantic double-deck Airbus A380 that went into service in 2006.

The car makers, with a freedom they had not enjoyed since the early days before aero engines predominated, grabbed the chance to build a new company.

Just days after the collapse, the receiver showed faith in the car business by financing a crucial media introduction in the south of France of a coach-built convertible named Corniche, signalling that Rolls-Royce was still the leading luxury car maker.

One of the most stylish convertibles Rolls-Royce had ever built, it was lauded by motoring writers as a symbol of brighter days to come. With technical developments and other refinements, including a turbo that made it the fastest open-top Rolls-Royce ever built, it became Corniche II, III and IV over a twenty-year production run – a notable example of the evolution philosophy.

The coachwork and that of a beautiful hard-top version was shaped at Mulliner Park Ward in west London, where skilled artisans performed their magic with flawless veneers and leather upholstery. Coach building was time consuming, each car taking almost six months to complete. A craftsman, for example, needed a week to fit the convertible top, work of such art that, when raised, the car appeared to be a coupé.

David Plastow, who had worked his way up from sales rep to CEO, had to persuade the workforce, shaken by the spectre of closure, that Rolls-Royce had a future.

Another new model in the works was Camargue, a big coach-built coupé with aircraft-style instrumentation, tagged the 'ultimate personal Rolls-Royce'.

The first Rolls designed from scratch to meet US safety legislation, the strength

Did you know?

Oil check: With the push of a button, the petrol gauge in Rolls-Royce Silver Shadows and later models became an oil-level check. This avoided drivers having to raise the bonnet and use the dipstick – a convenience that also avoided gentlemen getting grime on their cuffs.

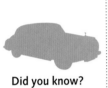

Did you know?
The climate control system of the Camargue – the most advanced in the world at that time, the 1970s – had the heating capacity of four radiators and the cooling power of thirty refrigerators.

▲▶ *The Corniche set the car makers on the road to recovery.*

◀ Based on the Silver Shadow, this stylish car was introduced as the Mulliner Park Ward two-door saloon. Later it became the Corniche coupé, which is much sought by collectors today.

of the bulky body was demonstrated by a single car passing all the crash tests, the roof giving only half an inch under a 3-ton load and the front successfully withstanding hitting a 100-ton concrete block head on at 30mph.

➤ The 1977 Silver Shadow II with loyal security guard.

Did you know?

To ensure paintwork durability, panels were taken to Australia to bake for days in the blistering sun of the outback, and to northern Scandinavia to see how they stood up to extended winter exposure.

The Camargue had a weighty $90,000 price tag at the US launch in 1976, making it the most expensive production car ever sold in America. Over eleven years, 526 were made and the final twelve, all painted white and fitted with additional luxury features, were priced at $175,000. Within a year or two they became collector cars, selling for upwards of $300,000.

The Silver Shadow saloon, which had superseded the beloved Silver Cloud in 1965, was the important bread-and-butter car. A radical change in design and engineering, it had no separate chassis frame but a monocoque steel body. The bonnet, boot lid and doors were aluminium alloy and the styling was some way from the glorious sweeping lines of the Cloud. Initially, purists said it was boxy and lacked elegance.

Notwithstanding, the Shadow hit most of the targets: lower and more compact than the Cloud, but with more space inside and impressive technical advancements. It was the first Rolls-Royce with a self-levelling independent front and rear suspension and back-up braking system.

Over twelve years, 2,000 changes were engineered into the car which, revamped in 1977, became Silver Shadow II. A long-

◀ *Camargue, an exclusive coach-built coupé named after the region in France that is noted for its wild horses, was a major styling departure for Rolls-Royce. Viewed by Crewe engineers as the best-riding luxury tank they produced in the 1970s, it was designed to appeal to Rolls-Royce enthusiasts with sporting instincts, who enjoyed driving a car with instrumentation redolent of an aeroplane cockpit.*

company promised would adjust to the heat of Death Valley or the cooler climes of Alaska without having to touch the switches. The freshened models, including Bentley versions, took sales to 3,000 in 1977 and a record 3,347 the following year.

The Shadow/Wraith series became the company's most commercially successful car, 31,714 being built over fifteen years.

THE SPIRIT EMERGES FROM THE SHADOWS

The Silver Spirit and extended wheelbase version Silver Spur in 1980 offered a new shape, slightly wider and lower than the Shadow, and improvements to steering, braking and suspension.

The objective was to make the Spirit and Spur both contemporary and elegant, incorporating supreme comfort and safety

wheelbase version was given a name from the past, Silver Wraith II. Both had powered rack-and-pinion steering, a new rear suspension to improve cornering and the Camargue's air conditioning, which the

and a feeling of well-being whether behind the wheel or lounging in the back.

With technical advances engineered into mark two and three versions, their lifespan stretched to seventeen years, until the Silver Seraph was introduced in 1998. The last Rolls-Royce saloon produced at Crewe, its softly rounded edges reflected the influence and beauty of the Silver Cloud.

Much of it was the work of chief stylist Graham Hull, who sought a modern interpretation of classic themes, giving the car Rolls-Royce hallmarks: presence and grace. He came up with a classic motor car.

▲ *First new body styles for fifteen years, flagships for the 1980s, the Silver Spirit and long-wheelbase Silver Spur.*

◄◄ *Highlighting Rolls-Royce engineering halfway through the twentieth century, the Silver Cloud and a de Havilland Comet, the world's first jet-powered airliner.*

◄ *Rolls-Royce Silver Shadow in a natural habitat – New York's Park Avenue.*

▼ The Shadow's more formal long-wheelbase sibling, the Silver Wraith II, suitable for a chauffeur or owner driver.

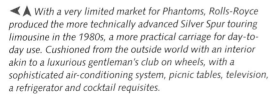

◀▲ *With a very limited market for Phantoms, Rolls-Royce produced the more technically advanced Silver Spur touring limousine in the 1980s, a more practical carriage for day-to-day use. Cushioned from the outside world with an interior akin to a luxurious gentleman's club on wheels, with a sophisticated air-conditioning system, picnic tables, television, a refrigerator and cocktail requisites.*

▲ *The Silver Seraph, the last saloon to be built at Crewe, in 1998.*

Did you know?

The security system in the Rolls-Royce Silver Shadow was patterned after pin-tumbler locks designed in Egypt 4,000 years ago to protect the tomb of a pharaoh. The odds against a thief successfully forging a key were claimed to be 24,000 to 1. For good measure, there was another security feature – a transmission lock automatically activated when the ignition key was removed.

◀ ▶ *The luxurious interior of the Seraph; a prime example of the peerless upholstery and veneer crafting of the skilled artisans at Crewe.*

The one place in the world where Rolls-Royce motor cars have been built outside England is Springfield, Massachusetts, a town with two other claims to fame: being the birthplace of basketball and home of the famous rifle. From 1921 to 1931, in order to meet increasing demand and take the strain off the home factory, Rolls-Royce made motor cars in Springfield – 1,703 Ghosts and 1,241 Phantoms.

Informed opinion has it that they were every bit as good as those made in England. One delighted owner wrote about 'driving my Springfield car from Philadelphia to Los Angeles and back, laden with wife, daughters and luggage'. He traversed road and prairie, dried up riverbeds and mountain passes, 'and the only attention the car required was fuel for the entire 6,627 miles'.

An early American owner was banker Pierpont 'If you have to ask the price, you can't afford it' Morgan. He was talking about a yacht, but his words also applied to Rolls-Royce.

Fifty-three engineers and supervisors, expert in every facet of the building of a

Did you know?

An American lady-owner had a duplicate set of instruments, apart from a steering wheel, fitted to the passenger compartment so that she could monitor the speed. Should the car be travelling faster than she considered prudent, she would shout at the chauffeur through a speaking tube that had been thoughtfully provided.

◄ *Springfield US-made Rolls-Royce.*

Did you know?

Rolls-Royce suspensions had a hydraulic self-levelling system to keep the car on an even keel. It even took into account the emptying of the fuel tank and was so strong, engineers claimed, it would take the weight of a fully grown African elephant on the boot without giving more than an inch. But this test was not advised by the company.

Rolls-Royce, travelled with their families from England, bringing blueprints and samples of every part at each stage of construction. They and locally recruited workers produced superb cars which, by 1925, had left-hand drive.

Celebrities who ordered Springfield Ghosts or Phantoms included Fred Astaire, America's sweetheart, the actress Mary Pickford, Mack Sennett, Greta Garbo and Irving Berlin. The Warner brothers owned several, one of which they gave to Al Jolson.

Charlie Chaplin owned a Ghost and one of the last Phantoms made in America; heavyweight champion Jack Dempsey had a 1924 Ghost; and Harold Lloyd, Howard Hughes and Gary Cooper all drove American-built Rolls-Royces. Even bootleggers in the south used a Springfield Rolls-Royce to outrun the 'Revenoo agents'. Henry Royce would have appreciated that.

The acclaimed quality of the Springfield cars, however, wasn't enough to keep the factory open. The great depression had much to do with its closing, but other factors played a part, like the heavy cost of buying the Brewster coach-building company.

Even though the plant had been profitable on about 300 cars a year, the operation was too small to meet tooling for new models.

Nonetheless, Springfield made a significant contribution to Rolls-Royce ownership in North America, and created a momentum that led to the US becoming the largest single Rolls-Royce market.

Did you know?

Rolls-Royce solemnly advised owners: 'Provided the engine is serviced and run on reputable fuel and oils with proper filtration and cooling, it will exceed 250,000 miles without the heads coming off for attention. Our engines regularly do just that.'

Say Brooklands or Le Mans and you automatically think Bentley – the great sporting motor cars that blasted the name into racing history, winning the famed Le Mans twenty-four-hour endurance race five times, four of the victories successively between 1927 and 1930.

The Bentley story reads like something out of *The Boy's Own Paper* – big, powerful 4- and 8-litre racers driven by a bunch of wealthy young men known as the Bentley Boys who would party into the night in London society, then roar down to Dover, catch the Channel ferry and drive furiously to Le Mans to race the cars through the afternoon and the night at insane speeds.

Their leader, Woolf Barnato, a millionaire playboy, won a bet that his Bentley Speed Six could not only outpace the French Blue Train express in a race from the Côte d'Azur, but would get him to London before the train reached Calais. Despite fog, heavy rain and blowing a tyre, he won by four hours.

The car was made by Walter Owen Bentley, a variant of Henry Royce with skates on. Like Royce, a former railway engineering apprentice, he worked on First World War aero engine design. He dreamed of making aggressive, robust racers masquerading as touring cars and started Bentley Motors in 1919, where he developed a four-cylinder, 3-litre engine, followed by a 6- and then 8-litre power. He also raced cars at the legendary Brooklands circuit – the cradle of British motor racing.

The 1929 depression triggered a chain of disastrous financial events for Bentley. His cars were expensive; so too the racing activities, and in 1931, on the heels of his

Did you know?
A prototype of the legendary 6.75-litre engine that powered Rolls-Royce motor cars for many years was run at full throttle for the equivalent of 40,000 miles without missing a beat.

Did you know?

'Bentleys are for the man who has won the race, but declines to wear the laurels', observed one enthusiast when asked why some preferred a Bentley to the higher-profile Rolls-Royce.

fifth Le Mans victory, the money ran out despite cash injections by Barnato, and Bentley Motors was bought by Rolls-Royce.

Bentley stayed on but was marginalised – an unfathomable misstep by the company. He left to design Aston Martin engines. The quality of the cars he had produced and the contribution he could have made to the design and testing of Rolls-Royce and Bentley cars would have made him the

➤ *Walter Owen Bentley, whose great engineering achievements earned him a special place in automotive and racing history.*

➤➤ *Glen Kidson and Woolf Barnato lead the victory parade at Le Mans, again.*

ideal engineering leader following Royce's death. Walter Bentley died in 1971. He was eighty-three.

From 1933 to the end of the century, Bentleys were built alongside Rolls-Royce, and for many years the cars were identical apart from the radiator shell and Flying B badging. However, the designers broke free now and again, to produce graceful styling like the Bentley Continental fastback, the fastest production saloon in the world, capable of sustaining 117mph.

It was the 1980s before Bentley recast its image and differentiated meaningfully from Rolls-Royce, producing sporting motor cars which appealed to drivers who wanted luxury and style but who felt they were too young for a Rolls-Royce.

The Bentley Turbo R – known as 'Crewe's missile' – a four-door saloon of phenomenal

◄ *Classic 1950s Bentley Continental – another car that makes collectors giddy.*

➤ *The Bentley TII saloon, which had a long production run with its near-identical sibling, the Silver Shadow.*

➤➤ *The Turbo R 'Crewe's missile' – the spectacular performance car that signalled the renaissance in the 1980s and told the motoring world that Bentley indeed was back.*

➤ *Classic hand-built cars. The great Bentley Continental name was given to a spectacular coach-built convertible, for drivers who desired the craftsmanship of the Rolls-Royce Corniche but opted for a lower profile.*

performance, accelerating its 2 tons from 0 to 60mph in just over six seconds, was launched in 1983. It was an international sensation.

The car recalled its racing heritage by covering over 140 miles in one hour, capturing the British endurance distance and other speed records. Bentley indeed was back!

Bentley became the 'sporting driver's car' again with a range of spirited performance cars, including the turbocharged Continental

Did you know?

Turbo engines were subjected to extended full-power tests that might have made those of many other cars blow up. At full throttle, the exhaust manifolds reached over 800°C, and glowed red hot. Silver-plated manifold nuts were used to ensure the threads did not seize. Engineers were proud that every engine in the Bentley Turbo R and the Rolls-Royce Flying Spur was able to take full-throttle acceleration from the moment it went on the road, though this was not recommended.

R coupé and the Brooklands, named after the famed motor racing circuit in Surrey.

For many years Rolls-Royce outsold Bentleys several to one, but that changed in the 1980s and 1990s. Bentley sales soared, overtaking Rolls-Royce when difficult economic times decreed that conspicuous consumption was out. Bentley outsold Rolls-Royce for several years in the late 1980s and 1990s, becoming a financial lifeline, but by itself could not stave off the underlying financial pressures that led to the company being sold and the marques going to different ownership.

Today, Bentley thrives, selling several thousand cars a year which are still made at the Crewe factory by craftsmen and women who have done this work there for many years, using their skills to make the finest motor car interiors in the world.

◄◄ *A glorious luxury convertible, the Bentley Azure, among the last of the 1995–2000 series was, at more than one third of a million dollars, the most expensive Bentley ever sold in America. The Azure underlined the dominance of the Bentley marque in the Crewe line-up.*

◄ *The magic of Brooklands, the cradle of British motor racing. Bentley named a new model in the 1980s the Brooklands and took it to what remained of the steep banking with a classic Bentley Le Mans racer that has seen more sweat, strain and racetrack mayhem than the saloon car drivers could imagine.*

Rolls-Royce owners, an eclectic lot, range from royalty and movie stars to lawyers, doctors, even Communist leaders, rewarding themselves with a car that speaks to their appreciation of the good things in life. Also strongly represented are the showbiz crowd whose artistic temperament can propel them to tabloid front pages.

Did you know?

Mrs Churchill Wylie decided to tour Africa in her 40/50hp limousine in the 1930s and, being unwilling to sacrifice home comforts, equipped the car with every modern convenience she could think of, including a wind-up gramophone, a bar, special cutlery and notepaper headed by a photograph of the car. She also fitted a washbasin in the boot.

Zsa Zsa Gabor, noted for her ability to collect husbands and eye-watering alimony, was out with her Corniche convertible when she got into a parking row with a cop. Pursuing an inadvisable course, she slapped him and ended up with three days in the slammer for assaulting a bastion of Beverly Hills law.

Rolls-Royce lovers can be amazingly generous at times. Elvis Presley peered through the window of a showroom in Memphis, liked the cars, and bought several to give to friends.

John Lennon had a psychedelic paint job done on his Phantom V limousine, triggering a management spasm, and Michael Caine recounts being thrown out of a showroom in London's Mayfair because a haughty salesman considered he was too unkempt to afford a Rolls-Royce.

When Rolls-Royce learned that a farmer in the Yorkshire Dales was ferrying pigs to market in the back of a Rolls-Royce, an emissary was dispatched to ask him to end this unthinkable practice. He was sent packing with a bit of agricultural logic: 'Pigs paid for it. Pigs'll ride in it.'

Henry Ford bought more than one Rolls, and explained that he had a duty to check out the competition as any manufacturer would.

A Texan removed the body from a Silver Ghost, substituted a full-sized model of his horse, with the steering wheel through its head, and adapted the controls so that, complete with Stetson and a six-shooter, he 'drove as he rode'.

Another Texan enthusiast liked to have cars from his collection in the house. He removed a 3-ton pipe organ from the family room of his Spanish-style home near San Antonio and put in garage doors to get his two favourite cars inside.

One of the world's richest men, the Sultan of Brunei, ruler of a small, oil-rich kingdom bordering Malaysia, loves Rolls-Royce and Bentley motor cars to the extent of buying 350, many built to unique specifications, including the only six-door limousine Rolls-Royce has ever made. His orders in the early 1990s for tens of millions of pounds worth of cars helped to keep the company afloat when it hit financial turbulence.

A cult leader in Oregon also became a heavy-hitting owner – not quite in the same league as the sultan, but giving it his best shot. Bhagwan Shree Rajneesh's 3,000 followers vowed to buy him 365 Rolls-Royces, one for every day of the year. They got as far as eighty-five, repainting many in garish colours, but everything fell apart when the US deported him.

Not all owners come from the ranks of the wealthy. In the 1980s a young British rubbish collector worked six days a week for five years to make enough money to buy a used Rolls-Royce.

A few leading Communists did not allow political principles to get in the way of comfort. Mao Tse Tung and Stalin each owned a Rolls-Royce and Lenin, father of the Russian Revolution, also selective in his egalitarian lifestyle, had nine.

Leonid Brezhnev, a later party chief, acquired several and the company would send an engineer to Moscow, even at the height of the Cold War, to service them. The top comrades, it seemed, knew how to protect a good capitalist investment.

Some Rolls-Royce owners are so proud of their cars that they have to tell the world. One licence plate announced 'I'm Rich'. Another sought to enhance a Corniche with 'You need a lot of bread to

▼ *'Good transportation for pigs,' says farmer.*

own a Rolls'. These were not old-school owners.

An American in what is euphemistically called the recreational pharmaceuticals industry was so delighted with his Silver Shadow that he proclaimed in big lettering on the boot: 'The Crowd Pleaser'. The special décor was finished off with a red, white and black checkerboard roof. It disappeared when the car was sold, but he did it again when he returned from a stay 'up the river'.

Enthusiasts will shell out a fortune for a special car. An English collector paid a record $2.86 million at auction in Palm Beach for a sibling of the 1907 Silver Ghost.

Even men of the cloth spring for a Rolls-Royce. The Right Reverend Dr Frederick Eikerenkoetter II – Revd Ike to his flock – was one of the most flamboyant preachers in New York. A powerful orator and a jolly man with a twinkle in his eye, he founded two churches and used several Rolls-Royce cars to spread his gospel of brotherly love and material success. The Revd Ike declared, 'Money is not the root of all evil. It is the absence of money that's evil.' His philosophy was: 'In my church, we teach aiming for riches. These damn cars are the nearest things I've come across to the chariots of The Lord.'

Only one American president, Woodrow Wilson, is on record as owning a Rolls-Royce. An early model, the car was a gift and is still running.

Some years ago a Californian owner was so infuriated by problems with his Silver Shadow that he hacked a hole in the roof, stuck in a lemon tree, spray-painted the slogan 'This Lemon was sold to me by Rolls-Royce' and trucked it up to Beverly

Did you know?
Some owners didn't mind being stared at. A Silver Spirit was seen in Ohio with a sticker on the rear bumper that read: *'I GOT THIS CAR FOR MY WIFE. HOW'S THAT FOR A TRADE?'*

by with somersaults and hand springs, he parked the vandalised car outside the Rolls-Royce showroom on Wilshire Boulevard. Crowds gathered, and the British owner of the business went ballistic. He had not even sold the man the car and understandably was upset when television crews showed up to add to the circus-like carnival that stopped traffic and generated publicity that placed Rolls-Royce executives in danger of a cardiac event.

Rolls-Royce owners do indeed march to their own drumbeat.

▲ One of the Bhagwan's garish paint jobs on a Silver Spur.

Hills on the 405, the most heavily trafficked freeway in America. Armed with a bullhorn, and accompanied by two attractive blondes in bikinis who entertained gaping passers-

With limited resources for new model investment, despite a strong order book, chief executive David Plastow, who had steered Rolls-Royce Motors to success in the 1970s, engineered a merger in 1980 with the venerable British conglomerate Vickers.

Famous for its guns, tanks, warships and aircraft, Vickers had made healthy profits for 100 years, often with the help of Rolls-Royce engines.

Plastow became chief executive of the expanded group, bringing with him a Rolls-Royce company that became a cash cow for Vickers in the 1980s, setting sales records with the new Silver Spirit and Silver Spur saloons, a Spur limousine and a revival of the Bentley marque. It also hit a milestone with the building of the 100,000th car.

Ten years along, however, sales collapsed as Britain and the US went into recession and Rolls-Royce plunged seriously into the red. Half the workforce had to go and Vickers itself came close to going under, having to fund restructuring costs running into tens of millions of pounds.

Production systems were modernised and, as the recession eased, business picked up with a range of new Bentleys, and the fastest Rolls-Royce cars in history, the turbocharged Flying Spur and Corniche S.

The economic reality, however, was that Rolls-Royce, making relatively few cars a year at great cost, struggled for development money and needed to be part of a larger car company. Vickers, spooked by the financial pain, put word out that it was open to offers.

A low-ball offer by BMW amounting to grand theft auto was rejected by Plastow, who also was reluctant to sell to a German company.

Did you know?

Sensors inside and outside a Rolls-Royce fed temperatures to the air-conditioning control centre, even taking into account the heat of the sun coming through the windscreen, a factor known as solar gain.

BMW tried again in 1998 after Plastow's retirement, triggering emotional protests from war veterans and some shareholders, who implored Vickers not to sell to the Germans. A consortium of enthusiasts tried to keep Rolls-Royce British but could not put financing together in time.

BMW's increased offer was accepted only to be outbid by Volkswagen, who weighed in with £479 million, which Vickers agreed to. This infuriated BMW and started a corporate brawl between the chairmen, BMW's Bernd Pischetsrieder and Volkswagen's Ferdinand Piech.

BMW had two trump cards. Pischetsrieder threatened to cancel a contract to supply engines and other parts for the new Rolls-Royce Silver Seraph – a result of lack of development funds at Crewe – if BMW did not get the right to make Rolls-Royce cars.

BMW also had business links to Rolls-Royce plc, the aerospace group which owned the Rolls-Royce name and RR badge, and had the power to decide who could make cars bearing the hallowed trademarks. It came down on BMW's side.

Volkswagen had assumed that Vickers had the right to permit it to make cars bearing the Rolls-Royce name and badge; Vickers thought so, too. That was not the case, it turned out.

Faced with having a car that could not be called Rolls-Royce and the handicap of not having an engine, Piech bowed to the inevitable and agreed to hand over the Rolls-Royce name to BMW in 2003.

BMW paid £40 million to the aerospace group for the rights to use the Rolls-Royce name on cars it would make at a factory in the south of England.

◀ The mantle passed in 2007 to a new Bentley powerhouse that would have thrilled the Bentley Boys – the Continental GTC, a high-performance, twelve-cylinder, all-wheel luxury convertible with a top speed north of 190mph.

Did you know?
All Rolls-Royce engines assembled at Crewe were built to a standard that required them to withstand 400 hours running at full power.

Did you know?
Measures taken to avoid extraneous sound in a Rolls-Royce included putting a man in the boot with his ear pressed to the carpet to find the source of a squeak as the car was driven over bumpy roads.

Despite being blindsided, Piech was magnanimous. His purchase included ownership of the radiator grille and Spirit of Ecstasy mascot, which he gracefully allowed BMW to use. He was acknowledged in the press as the only statesman in the whole acrimonious affair.

Volkswagen came away with Bentley and the Crewe factory, which it updated, spending tens of millions of pounds, and continued to make Rolls-Royce cars for five years, until BMW assumed the name for its cars.

A stylish range of Bentley 'sporting motor cars' was introduced, benefiting from Volkswagen's enormous engineering heft and unrivalled luxurious interiors for which Crewe craftspeople are renowned. In the first decade of the twenty-first century, Bentley sales soared to an unprecedented 10,000 cars a year.

The splitting of the companies turned out to be a boon for both marques, providing them an assured future.

The new BMW-owned company, Rolls-Royce Motor Cars Ltd, built a factory at Goodwood in Sussex, aiming to produce a car of 'understated elegance, modernism and perfect proportions' that would be appropriate to the line of flagships bearing a distinguished lineage. There could be only one name: Phantom.

The revered name had adorned six coach-built limousines covering seventy-five years of the history of Henry Royce's company, the first one being built at Derby in 1925.

Design teams worked for five years on the first BMW Rolls-Royce, which left Goodwood in January 2003, the moment it could legally sell a car bearing the name and famous badge.

They came up with a large car fronted by an enormous grille, which the *New York Times* likened to a caricature.

The profile was graceful, with hints of Rolls-Royce coachwork of the past. The *Daily Telegraph* described it as 'A stylish collision between cool Bavarian and traditional gentleman's club'.

Superbly engineered, powerful and easy to drive, the 2½-ton, 19ft-long Phantom leaped quietly from rest to 60mph in 5.7 seconds, topping out at 149mph.

Journalists praised its comfort, performance, handling and technical excellence. The *New York Times* noted that the 6.75-litre engine stemmed from BMW's 6-litre V-12, with most of the running gear derived or borrowed from the BMW 7.

The media was less than enthusiastic about its appearance, however. *Automobile* magazine's design editor opined: 'Incongruously gigantic, mounted on brutal wheels that could have come from a

◄► Phantoms are exported to more than fifty countries. The US is the leading market, followed by Britain and China.

Did you know?

The famed Peninsula Hotel in Hong Kong has made money for years with a fleet of ten cars providing guests the opportunity to arrive and depart in Rolls-Royce style. Japanese tourists, especially, happily pay a hefty premium to be greeted at the airport by a liveried chauffeur and wafted serenely through the maelstrom to Kowloon.

◀ ▶ *The spacious and beautifully finished Phantom interior.*

◄ *Phantom extended wheelbase.*

➤ *Phantom GCC Limited Edition.*

Phantom convertible and Phantom coupé. The convertible carried a price tag of £274,100 before tax in 2011. Below, the coupé version.

The armoured Phantom, built for those 'seeking the highest levels of personal protection'.

The battery-driven experimental electric Phantom which made its first appearance in 2011.

102EX

Wehrmacht vehicle ... a bit bizarre for what traditionally has been an understated and subtly elegant marque.'

'A Soviet staff car', was the verdict in a *Wall Street Journal* feature called 'The Ugly Cars'.

Unquestionably, the Phantom, and models that have followed, are the most technologically advanced cars to carry the Rolls-Royce name; their luxury and superb engineering have been applauded by owners and the media.

By the summer of 2007 Phantom offered a more spacious variant, nearly a foot longer, costing a quarter of a million pounds. An armoured Phantom also became available, followed by a coupé and a convertible.

In 2010 another distinguished name, Ghost, was called up from the past for a slightly smaller car, packing stunning performance. A new 6.6-litre turbocharged V12 engine generating a prodigious 563hp propelled this luxurious projectile from 0–60 in under five seconds. The before tax price, £165,000, was an 'affordable ticket to the club', considering the Phantom's £235,000.

It was joined in late 2011 by a long-wheelbase Ghost with similar sizzle.

An experimental electric Phantom, the 102EX, also appeared in 2011. Powered by a lithium-ion battery pack and two electric motors, it went on a world tour to seek feedback from customers and dealers.

The new company, in 2003, had hoped to sell 1,000 Phantoms a year, but the early going was difficult and it took three years to reach the target. In the recovery period following the 2009 international financial meltdown, however, the expanded model range doubled worldwide sales to 2,711 in

◄ *Phantom speeds into the night 'not so much cutting through the air as battering it aside', as one British automotive writer observed about Rolls-Royce styling. But, of course, doing it with panache and serenity.*

2010 and 1,591 in the first half of 2011. With increasing orders for special-feature 'bespoke cars', the company announced plans to expand the factory.

BMW and Volkswagen have paid enormous respect to the heritage of the two great companies they acquired, providing engineering and financial resources to ensure a future for distinguished marques that looked questionable in the mid-nineties. They have also done something else that is dear to the hearts of England: they have preserved time-honoured craftsmanship in natural materials and are committed to the principle of getting every detail right.

Henry Royce, Charles Rolls and Walter Bentley would be very pleased about that.

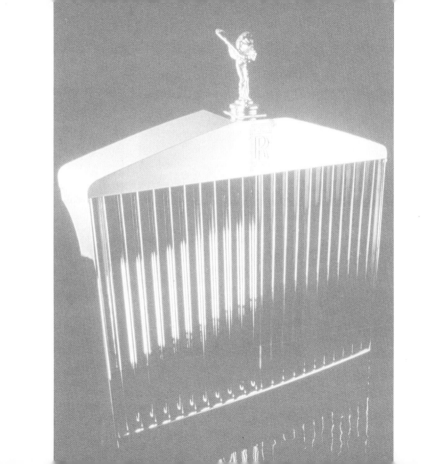

Other titles available in this series

THE WELLINGTON BOMBER STORY

MARTIN W. BOWMAN

■ ISBN 978 0 7524 6193 9

CHRIS FRAME & RACHELLE CROSS

THE QE2 STORY

■ ISBN 978 0 7524 5094 0

JOHN CHRISTOPHER

THE LONDON BUS STORY

■ ISBN 978 0 7524 5084 1

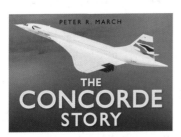

PETER R. MARCH

THE CONCORDE STORY

■ ISBN 978 0 7509 3980 5

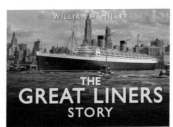

WILLIAM H. MILLER

THE GREAT LINERS STORY

■ ISBN 978 0 7524 6452 7

CHRIS FRAME & RACHELLE CROSS

THE QM2 STORY

■ ISBN 978 0 7524 5092 6

The History Press

Visit our website and discover thousands of other History Press books.
www.thehistorypress.co.uk